Contents

Introduction

Backpacking is an exhilarating and liberating way to explore the world, as well as a horizon-expanding opportunity to meet people from all corners of the globe.

Understandably you or a nail-biting parent may have a few concerns about the risks involved, but there's no reason why you shouldn't be able to avoid any major disasters. This book doesn't claim to have the solution to every tricky situation that you may come across on your travels, nor is it meant to scare or discourage you. Rather it will simply help you think more carefully about how to make your trip a safe one. Most travellers don't encounter anything worse than the occasional hairy but harmless spider, so armed with this book and a bit of common sense your trip should be the experience of a lifetime – for all the right reasons. Bon voyage!

Before you go

Research your destination thoroughly

... by reading guide books and Internet sites and talking to others who have been on a similar trip. Pay particular attention to local climates and seasons, traditions, diseases and potential dangers to be aware of. Being informed about the countries you are going to will prepare you for what's ahead and give you confidence. Useful websites are listed at the back of this book in the resources section.

Learn a few words in the local language

... of the countries you intend to visit, especially if you are travelling to areas where English is not widely spoken, such as many places in South America. It is particularly useful to know how to ask for directions, where the toilet is, how much something costs, and for help in case of an emergency. Local people are likely to be more receptive if you make the effort to learn basic greetings such as 'Hello', 'Goodbye' and 'Pleased to meet you'.

Consider taking a first-aid and self-defence course

... before you go. There are also courses run year round specifically designed for those about to go backpacking, covering aspects such as how to prepare for your trip, personal safety, medical issues and what to do in an emergency. These courses aren't just designed to reassure paranoid parents: you will probably find that just knowing how to deal with a threatening situation, or what to do in the event of a spider bite, will dispel any apprehension you may be feeling about your trip, especially if you are travelling alone. However, you should never expose yourself to potential danger presuming you could deal with it just because you have this knowledge.

Visit the Foreign and Commonwealth Office website

... for updates on the political, economic and cultural situation in the countries you are planning to visit, as these can change very rapidly and it's important to be up to speed about what's going on before your departure.

Ensure that your passport is valid

... for at least six months after your expected return date. If you need to apply for or renew your passport, find out the time scale for processing your application and make sure you submit it in plenty of time to receive your up-to-date passport before your planned departure date. The UK passport service advise that they aim to process and return postal applications within three weeks, but this may be delayed so do allow plenty of extra time.

TRAVEL TRIVIA

99.985 per cent of all overseas travellers make it home safely.

Arrange adequate travel insurance

... before you go. Remember that the cheapest policy available may not necessarily be the best one. You need to check that your policy will cover not only the areas that you plan to visit, but also any activities that you intend to participate in whilst on your travels; for example, scuba diving or trekking. Your insurance company must be notified of any changes you make to your trip, such as extending the length, otherwise any claims you make may be invalid. Familiarise yourself with the policy before you go, ensuring you are aware of the excess, exactly what you are covered for and the emergency telephone number for contacting the company for assistance from abroad.

Always carry photocopies of your important documents

... including your passport, insurance policy and flight tickets, in a different place to the originals, and ensure that you leave copies with someone at home.

As an extra security measure, scan these documents into the computer and e-mail them to yourself at a web-based account (such as Hotmail) so they are ready to print out should you require them.

Check if there are airport taxes

In some countries there are airport taxes payable on leaving the country. You will need to check this in advance and budget for it, since if you are unable to pay you will not be allowed to check in for your flight.

TRAVEL FAUX PAS

IN MEXICO IT IS CONSIDERED POLITE TO PLACE YOUR MONEY IN THE CASHIER'S HAND RATHER THAN ONTO THE COUNTER WHEN PAYING FOR GOODS.

Check you are able to access online banking

... in the countries you are planning to visit. Online banking can be very useful for monitoring your spending while away and transferring money between accounts, but do make sure that you make other provisions in case you are unable to access it.

Take some traveller's cheques and US dollars with you

Traveller's cheques can be replaced if they are lost or stolen and most places around the world accept US dollars, so it is a good idea to take a supply of notes in various denominations. This can be especially useful when passing through a lot of countries within a short period of time as it is often costly and time-consuming to keep changing money to the local currency.

Keep phone numbers safe

Take a note of the number that you can call
from abroad if you need to cancel your credit
card. Keep it somewhere safe and separate
from your credit card, in case your wallet is
lost or stolen. Remember that 0800 numbers
that you dial from within the UK will not
always work from abroad.

Visit the nurse at your local GP surgery

... at least six weeks before you depart to get any necessary vaccinations and anti-malarial tablets. Take a record of which injections you have had with you on your trip.

TRAVEL FAUX PAS

For religious reasons, a strict male Muslim will be uncomfortable if a woman offers her hand to shake by way of greeting. Women can press their hands to their hearts as an alternative greeting.

Take your prescription and a letter from your doctor

... if you are carrying any medication with you. This will be essential in case of loss or suspicious customs officers. Be aware that some medicines prescribed in the UK may be illegal in other countries, so check this before you go.

Take contraception supplies

... as some countries may not offer good
access to these. Remember that vomiting and
diarrhoea can negate the effects of the birth
control pill so use alternative contraception
for at least seven days after a bout of food
poisoning or other illness.

Always carry a medical kit

... in your backpack. How much you put in it should depend on the medical facilities available in the countries you are visiting, and what you plan to do whilst there. Obviously if you are planning to go trekking or travel through very rural areas, your kit should be fairly substantial. You can buy ready-made kits from St John's Ambulance or the British Red Cross, or you can make up your own. Here are a few items that no traveller should be without, but this list is by no means exhaustive so seek advice before you go, and take into account your own situation.

Medical kit checklist

- An easy-to-read first aid manual
- Antiseptic cream and/or wipes
- Plasters, a roll of cloth bandage and gauze strips
- Scissors
- Anti-diarrhoea tablets
- Painkillers
- Safety pins
- Water-purifying tablets
- Insect repellent
- Sunscreen
- Lip protection

Remember that the risk of theft whilst travelling is higher

... than it is at home so be selective about what you pack and try to avoid taking expensive electrical and digital devices. For example, if you enjoy listening to music to while away the time on long journeys, then you could always buy a cheap MP3 player instead of taking your 60 GB iPod.

A mobile phone can be really useful

... in an emergency, but remember that it is likely to be expensive to use abroad and could fall prey to theft. If you do plan to take a mobile phone with you, check that it will work in the countries you are planning to visit. You may need to contact your network provider to have the phone unlocked for use abroad.

Invest in a good quality padlock

... so that you can secure your backpack when travelling or when leaving belongings in your hostel. Although this won't prevent a determined thief from slashing your bag to reach the contents, it will act as a deterrent to would-be opportunists. It is also possible to purchase wire meshes specifically designed to fit over your backpack and make it 'slash proof'.

CASE STUDY

When we were backpacking around South Korea, hardly any of the bank machines accepted foreign cards, except for a few in foreign hotels in Seoul. Not having any cash can be annoying when you can't buy dinner, but it can also leave you stranded. One time we hoped we could simply go to a bank and get an advance that way, but we hadn't realised it was a bank holiday, and we had to catch a bus to get us back to Seoul to make an important connection. In the end we found a tourist office that was open, and I managed to persuade the woman working there to look up the day's exchange rate online and exchange a twenty-dollar (US) note for Korean currency.

Jennifer Barclay

Pack a whistle or rape alarm

These can be used in case of attack or if you need to draw attention to yourself, for example if you get separated from your group on a trek.

IN MALAYSIA YOU CAN CAUSE GREAT OFFENCE BY USING YOUR INDEX FINGER TO POINT AT PEOPLE OR OBJECTS.

Remember to pack some warm and waterproof clothes

... even when going to a country with a predominantly hot climate. In some areas, such as Asia, there are extended rainy seasons so it's always best to find out about seasonal particularities and local climate when planning your trip.

Leave your itinerary with someone at home

... including details of all flights and any accommodation that you have pre-booked.

TRAVEL FAUX PAS

IN SHANGHAI IT IS NOT CONSIDERED RUDE TO SPIT IN PUBLIC, SO DON'T BE AFFRONTED IF PEOPLE SPIT MID-CONVERSATION.

Carry a sleeping bag or inner sheet

This is especially important if backpacking around rural regions, even if you are staying in hotels. Beds are not always clean, and you might need to put the sheet over your head to keep insects away.

Traveller's checklist

- Passport
- Photocopies of important documents
- Record of injections
- Prescriptions for any medicines you are carrying
- Emergency phone numbers
- Insurance details
- Traveller's cheques and US dollars
- First aid kit
- Padlock and key
- Small torch
- Whistle or rape alarm
- Contraception
- Waterproof clothing
- Inner sheet or sleeping bag
- European Health Insurance Card
- Map and compass
- Slash-proof wire mesh for backpack

On the move

Travel in pairs or groups

This is always advisable, especially for female travellers. Lone travellers lugging heavy bags are easy prey for corrupt characters and are their primary targets.

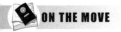

Keep in touch with people at home

... and always let someone know when you are moving on to a different country. Try to warn them if there will be a period when you won't be able to call or write, such as when you are going on a boat trip or jungle trek, so they won't worry.

Remember that aeroplane tickets have your credit card number printed on them

... so if your ticket is lost or stolen you will need to contact both the airline and your credit card company, and may even have to cancel your card.

TRAVEL TRIVIA

Studies have shown that
flying is 15 times safer than
driving and 300 times safer
than riding a motorbike.

When arriving at airports, be wary of 'porters'

... who offer to carry your bags for you. They may charge you a lot of money for taking your bags only a few metres, or even steal your luggage. People who approach you to ask what you are doing and if you need help could end up demanding money for the 'favour' they have just done for you, or even take you to a quiet area where they plan to rob you. You should also be wary of people who offer to negotiate prices of accommodation or transport for you. They may only be offering to help because they have an agreement to get a cut of the inflated charge that will be offered, so you could end up paying a higher rate.

Do not agree to carry anything

... for someone you don't know. If you are approached to do this at an airport or a train or bus station, say no and report it immediately to a member of staff.

Be wary of taxi drivers

... who tell you that there are no buses available, due to a strike, festival etc. Always double-check this with a reliable source – the information desk or tourist office, for example – as this is often used as a ploy to entice you to use their more expensive transport, rather than take the bus.

This also applies if you are stopped by a well-dressed stranger in the street who asks where you are going. It is commonplace in a lot of major foreign cities to be told that the attraction you are going to see is closed. Don't take their word for it; go and find out yourself. These people are often fraudsters who will take you to a different attraction and charge you exorbitant prices for the privilege.

Always use registered taxis

The car should be clearly marked and the driver should have identification on display inside the car. Make sure you agree the fare with the driver before getting in. If you can, pre-book your transport and reach an agreement about the fare when you make the booking.

Keep the doors locked and windows closed

... while driving a hire car through cities and towns. However, keep them unlocked/ open when driving on motorways in case of an accident, as you may need to escape quickly from the vehicle. It will also make it easier for a rescue team to get you out of the car in the event that you are trapped or unconscious inside.

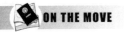

When driving alone, never stop to assist drivers

... who have broken down at the side of the road, as it may be a trap. If you are not alone and you do decide to offer assistance, make sure you lock your car and place the key discreetly in a secure pocket. If there is no evidence of injury, it is usually better not to stop in these situations, especially on isolated roads, but do alert the police or other authority when you reach the next town.

Never hitchhike or accept lifts from strangers

... particularly when travelling alone. Similarly, never pick up anyone who is hitchhiking or touting for a lift.

TRAVEL FAUX PAS

IN MUMBAI THE BECKONING HAND MOTION USED COMMONLY IN THE WEST FOR 'COME HERE' IS USED FOR SIGNALLING TO SERVANTS OR PROSTITUTES AND IS SEEN AS VERY RUDE.

Be aware of the quality of roads

... which may not be as good as what you are accustomed to and watch out for hazards such as potholes and dry river beds. Do not attempt difficult roads or off-road driving without a four-wheel drive vehicle.

Never leave your backpack unattended

When travelling on buses that require you to store your luggage in a compartment underneath the vehicle, try to keep an eye on the compartment and the people around it until they close the hatch.

When travelling in a taxi, take all your belongings in the back seat with you; there have been reported cases of unscrupulous drivers speeding off before the passenger can retrieve their luggage from the boot.

Put any important documents in a waterproof bag

... in case your backpack gets wet. This includes your passport, tickets, any prescriptions and so on. You can buy these bags from a specialist camping shop, but a zip lock bag will do just as well.

Do not cross any borders in another person's vehicle

... because if they have illegal items in their luggage, you will be held accountable as well.

TRAVEL FAUX PAS

NEVER ATTEMPT TO ATTRACT THE ATTENTION OF A PARISIAN WAITER BY CALLING OUT 'GARÇON', AS THIS IS THE EQUIVALENT OF HAILING AN ENGLISH WAITER WITH CRIES OF 'COME HERE, BOY'.

Be cooperative and friendly

... when it comes to immigration officers and border check points. Don't worry: they are usually individuals who enjoy wielding power over tourists, so if you don't give them any reason to get defensive then the whole process will be much easier.

Book accommodation ahead of time

... when you know that you are going to be arriving late in a city. Ask if they will organise transport from the airport/station. It is always a good idea to avoid being out at night in an unfamiliar city, laden down with all your luggage. If you haven't managed to book anything in advance, ask staff at the airport or station to recommend a place nearby and, if possible, ask them to phone to see if there are vacancies.

In your accommodation

Familiarise yourself with the fire exits

... and the location of fire alarms and extinguishers when you arrive at your accommodation, in case of emergency.

CASE STUDY

While I was backpacking around Canada, ten of us from one of the hostels I stayed in decided to stick around town for a couple of months and moved into a big old house. One day I noticed my coat was missing from the rail in the hallway – trouble was, I'd left my wallet in the pocket. The coat turned up a few days later in the basement, minus the wallet. I lost the last of my cash and had to cancel all my cards and get new ones. My housemates were all very sympathetic and more than one offered to pay my rent while I sorted things out with the bank; but one of them had stolen from me. It's worth remembering that those you live with may also receive visitors, who could be even less honorable with a stranger's belongings. Most new friendships you make will be genuine, but don't take chances – there may be the occasional fellow backpacker who will make the most of just such an opportunity.

Carol Baker

Always put valuables in the hostel safe

... when possible, and get a receipt for what you have deposited. If what you have left is of a very high value, it might be an idea to check the insurance limit and policy that the hostel offers. If you are planning on staying in beach huts, especially in Asia, make sure you pack a padlock and key for your hut door. Often hut (or 'bungalow') owners don't provide them.

Don't leave your hostel or hotel windows open

... when you go out or when you are in the bathroom, especially if you are staying on the ground floor or if your windows are easily accessible from the fire escape or other rooms/balconies. Even when you are in your room it is best to lock any valuables or important documents in the safe or inside your backpack.

Avoid staying in dorms

... when travelling in India and poorer parts of Asia, as they often attract thieves and drug addicts and the security is very poor. The cost of living in these countries is usually so low that for very little money, you can stay in more comfortable places with private rooms that are much safer. As a general rule, dorms are safe in many travelling hotspots such as Australia, but always take sensible precautions for your own safety and the security of your possessions. If you ever feel uneasy, speak to staff about moving rooms, or find another hostel.

Leave the window slightly open

... if there is a gas source such as a radiator in your room, so that if there is a fault the gas can escape and there will be a constant supply of fresh air.

TRAVEL FAUX PAS

DIRECT EYE CONTACT CAN BE SEEN AS AGGRESSIVE IN LATIN AMERICA.

Always leave your room key at reception

... as losing it, either by theft or by accident, will incur a charge. It is one less thing to worry about when you are out and about if your key is safely back at your accommodation. Just remember to check what time reception opens and closes!

Investigate the luggage storage system

... at the local train station if you are camping, or staying at a hostel where you are unsure if the security is adequate. Some stations offer lockers or a staffed storage facility. This can also be useful if you are travelling around a lot in one area and want somewhere safe to leave bags that you don't need.

Out and about

Buy a cheap wallet to take out with you

... on a daily basis. You can use it to carry just a few notes of a low denomination for paying for small items like drinks on street stalls, and also to hand over in case of being mugged or robbed.

TRAVEL TRIVIA

One in seven British travellers on overseas trips don't have any insurance.

Invest in a money belt

They may not be the most stylish items around but you can buy very thin and inconspicuous ones that are comfortable and secure and can easily hold your money, cards and passport. Wearing one means that you won't need to check your bag anxiously every half an hour to make sure your wallet is still there. If you have to take anything out of your money belt, do so in a secure and private place, such as a toilet cubicle, to avoid drawing attention to it and exposing it to any nearby thieves.

Always be careful when using the services of moneychangers

... especially those that offer a better rate than the majority, as this is often a ploy that deceitful businesses use to attract custom. Take a calculator to work out how much money you should be receiving, and when the money is handed over to you count it carefully a couple of times and make sure you get a receipt. It is best to do a few transactions over the period that you are in the country for, rather than changing a large amount of money at one time. You should always use official moneychangers and keep all receipts, as you may have to prove that you obtained your local currency legally.

Always wear appropriate clothing

... for the country you are visiting. As well as demonstrating respect for the country and its culture, this will help to make you less conspicuous and therefore less of a target for harassment, theft and unwanted attention. For example, when visiting Muslim countries, it is a good idea for female travellers to cover their hair, legs and shoulders and to dress modestly. A sarong is a very useful item to take with you, as it can double as a shawl, a skirt or a towel when needed.

Turn to look behind you at regular intervals

... if you go out walking, either in the city or the countryside, so that you are able to visualise the route for the return journey.

TRAVEL
FAUX PAS

IN MUSLIM COUNTRIES IT IS CONSIDERED RUDE TO USE YOUR LEFT HAND TO EAT, PASS FOOD, WIPE YOUR MOUTH OR EXCHANGE MONEY.

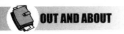

Carry a business card from your hotel/hostel

... giving the address in the native language: this way any driver should be able to take you there, and locals will be able to point you in the right direction if you are lost.

Ask before you get your camera out

... in certain places. In many countries, it is considered rude or even suspicious to take photos of people or certain buildings and monuments. In Egypt it is also common for local people to get in shot just as you are about to take a photo, and then demand that you pay them a fee for having captured their image.

Ask to see some identification

... if you are ever suspicious of anyone who says they are a police officer and asks you for information, a large sum of money or to search your room or possessions. If they refuse to show ID but remain insistent, politely offer to walk with them to the police station to sort the matter out so that you can verify their status: never get into a car with anyone you are unsure about.

Avoid public toilets in big cities

... as they can be dangerous and unhygienic. If you need to use the toilet when you're out and about, try to find a busy fast food restaurant or department store.

TRAVEL FAUX PAS

IF AN INDIAN SHAKES HIS HEAD, HE OR SHE MEANS YES.

Do not give out your address

... personal details or financial information to strangers. In Asia it is quite common for people to chat to you and ask what might seem quite personal questions about where you live and what job you do. This is usually quite harmless: they are most likely just being friendly or they may be trying to work out what your social status is. However, if you feel pressured by anyone who starts chatting to you and then asks for your address simply give a false address and move away quickly.

Be selective about who you approach

... if you need help with directions or other information: it is usually safer to approach parents with their children, policemen and shop or bank workers.

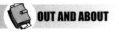

Avoid demonstrations and protests

If the police get involved they probably won't discriminate about who they arrest or upon whom they use reasonable force.

Wear inexpensive jewellery

... that you can pick up during your travels, rather than expensive accessories that might draw attention to you and make you a target for thieves.

Be extra vigilant in places like crowded markets

... and train and bus stations. Wherever there are lots of tourists, the pickpockets always follow.

TRAVEL FAUX PAS

BE CAREFUL HOW YOU INTERPRET A 'FRIENDLY' SMILE IN THE FAR EAST: IT COULD ALSO BE USED TO COVER UP EMBARRASSMENT OR ANGER.

Clasp your pockets shut

... with a safety pin if you are visiting notorious pickpocketing areas. This way no one can get to your belongings without you noticing in plenty of time. You can also buy combat trousers with deep pockets that close with buttons or zips, allowing you to store more items comfortably and without having to carry an extra bag.

CASE STUDY

Beware of the word 'pub' in Tokyo. Desperate for a drink a couple of friends and I went into a place called 'Pub Enjoy'. It seemed harmless enough, if not a little strange. There were lots of men in suits singing karaoke in front of what looked like some Christmas tree lights. We ordered a small beer each. Then a Chinese girl in a ball gown came over to talk to us. Next the owner was coming to our table. She spoke no English at all but insisted on handing us cashew nuts one by one. After a while the penny was dropping that this was not an average pub. So we tried to leave and that's where the sting came. They wanted to charge us 10,000 yen (fifty pounds) for each beer! The word 'Pub' generally indicates that a place is a hostess bar in Japan and the prices are very high. So my advice is to stick to izakayas (Japanese pubs) where the food and beer will not cost you a month's rent.

David Jones

Use a safety pin

... if you don't have a lock for the backpack that you carry around during the day. Clasp the zip together – this can delay potential thieves for those vital few seconds it may take you to realise someone is trying to open your bag.

Wear your daypack on your front

... especially when standing in queues or wandering around busy places, such as markets and tourist attractions. Some thieves will cut bags with knives so that the contents are easily accessible, but if yours is always in your line of sight, this can be avoided.

Be careful if anyone knocks into you on the street

Check that all your belongings are safe and secure.

TRAVEL FAUX PAS

IN INDIA WEARING THE COLOURS GREEN, RED OR YELLOW IS THOUGHT TO BRING GOOD LUCK, WHEREAS BLACK AND WHITE ARE CONSIDERED UNLUCKY.

Attach a bell to your backpack

... especially the zip, to alert you to anyone that may be interfering with it while you are on public transport or in a hostel dorm. You can buy a small one from an arts and craft shop, or even a pet shop (you may have to buy the collar it's attached to!).

Be aware of your surroundings

If, for example, you see two people separating directly in front of you without seeming to say goodbye to each other, be prepared for the possibility that it may be a coordinated robbery attempt. The best thing to do would be to change direction or head to a safe place, like a café or a shop.

Keep a close eye on your belongings

... if anybody stops you on the street to ask for directions, a lighter etc., and don't let the person stand too close. Use your instincts; if a situation doesn't feel right or you feel uncomfortable in any way, keep moving until you find an area where you feel safer. Don't be embarrassed about shaking your head and not stopping if someone asks for something as you are walking along. If they are genuine, they will find somebody else to ask for help.

Stay as far away as you can

... if there is a fight on the street, in a bar or in a shop. By keeping your distance you will avoid getting involved and risking injury. If it is a fight staged by thieves to serve as a distraction, this may save your valuables from getting stolen.

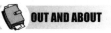

TRAVEL TRIVIA

The most frequent cause of
death among backpackers
is traffic accidents.

Be wary if anybody spills anything on you

Refuse their help if they offer to wipe your dirtied clothes or luggage, and never put your bags down to try and clean it up yourself. Go to a nearby bathroom to sort it out in safety. When walking next to a road, always carry any hand-held or shoulder bags on the side away from the street. A common method of theft is for motorcyclists to drive up behind you and the passenger to grab your bag.

Ask where the dangerous parts are

... if you are visiting a city, so that you can avoid them, especially after dark. Hostel staff or other backpackers should be able to help. When walking around at night, steer clear of streets with little or no lighting and walk as near to the road as you can as you pass doorways and alley-way entrances.

Never be pressured into making decisions

... especially when it comes to paying out money or agreeing to go somewhere. If you are unsure, say you will think about it and come back. An honest person will not try to force you to do anything. If you say that you don't have any money, that will usually make a pushy street vendor or salesperson back down. Be wary of vendors who try to entice you to their stalls with cries of 'Just looking?' or similar. Chances are you will struggle to leave the stall without purchasing a leather handbag, Persian rug or other item you had no original intention of buying.

It is advisable not to buy wildlife souvenirs

... such as ivory, artefacts made from animal pelts, shells or any flora or fauna products. Some items may be banned from international trade, which means you may not be able to take them out of the country you are visiting. You could also risk confiscation, a fine or even criminal prosecution when you reach UK customs.

Watch out for hidden extras in restaurants

If you are eating out and food or drink that you have not ordered appears on the bill, draw it to the waiter's attention and ask for the manager if there is a problem. Sometimes restaurants will give you free shots or aperitifs, but if you are in doubt it is worth double-checking if the waiter brings you anything you aren't expecting, as you may have to pay for the items later. Hidden extras are especially common in Spain and other southern European countries.

Be careful when drinking alcohol

You will be less aware of what is going on around you if you are drunk and may inadvertently put yourself in danger. Remember, if you have an accident or are injured as a result of being under the influence of alcohol or drugs, your travel insurance will most likely be invalidated, meaning you will have to pay medical fees and any other costs incurred as a result.

Always watch your drinks being prepared

... when in a bar, and never let them out of your sight. If you want to go outside and are not permitted to take your drink out of the bar – when going to have a cigarette in America for example – finish your drink first. Never ask anyone you don't know well to watch your drink.

Active awareness

Be aware of the environment

... you are entering when visiting an area of natural beauty. Don't let your guard down just because you are in what you perceive to be a well-maintained and safe facility – wild animals are essentially unpredictable and dangerous creatures, so never take any risks and remember at all times that you are in their territory. As a general rule, it is inadvisable to get out of your vehicle, to feed wild animals and to take picnics and other foodstuffs, especially fresh fruit, as this can attract the animals.

Find out locally if it is safe to swim

... before going in the sea, and check what the pollution levels, tide patterns and lifeguard provision are like. Don't swim in the sea when it is particularly rough, and be extra careful during the monsoon season, as strong currents are more frequent at this time.

Keep your belongings guarded

If you are swimming in the sea or going for a walk along the beach and need to leave some possessions on the sand, ask somebody nearby to keep an eye on them. Families or elderly couples are often a reliable choice for this. You should never leave valuables unattended, though, and if you know that you will be away from your towel, leave your camera, room key and wallet at the hostel. If you need to take cash, keep it to a minimum and consider burying it in the sand in a plastic bag or wallet. Remember where you've left it, though!

Find out about any potential swimming hazards

... before entering the water. Bear in mind that your fellow bathers could include other local inhabitants such as crocodiles, hippos, sharks or other dangerous creatures that should be kept at a great distance at all times. If you are in any doubt, don't swim.

Stick to chlorinated pools

... if you fancy going for a swim inland so as to avoid contracting infections that may be present in fresh water. In most African countries you are in danger of picking up bilharzia if you paddle or swim in freshwater rivers, lakes, ponds or irrigation canals. Bilharzia is a disease caused by parasitic worms, which can lead to serious liver, bladder and kidney damage.

Wear appropriate footwear

... at all times and avoid walking anywhere barefoot. In many tropical countries there are parasites which may enter your body through the soles of your feet. If you are trekking in the jungle or savannah you should wear walking boots and thick socks, even when it is very hot, to avoid the risk of snakebites and injuries from thorns. Remember to check for ticks after walking through long grass and leeches after wading through water. You should also wear sandals while walking along the seashore as coral cuts can take weeks to heal because coral contains chemicals that prevents the blood from clotting properly.

Keep dry whenever you are out trekking

... in the country, as hypothermia can set in quickly if you are cold and wet. Always take waterproof clothing and a thermal vest with you, even if it looks clear and sunny, as the weather can be very changeable in the tropics and also at high altitudes. It is also a good idea to take a couple of spare items of clothing in your bag – for example, a pair of socks and a T-shirt – just in case you do get wet and need to change.

CASE STUDY

I was travelling through Morocco when I broke out in terrible itchy hives all over my body. Since they were getting worse each day, I decided to go to a doctor in a town near the beach where I was camping. The doctor was extremely tense as I sat in his dingy office telling him about the hives and when I started to pull up my long-sleeved shirt to show him my red forearm, he shouted, 'Stop!' He turned away from me, closed his eyes, and with his hand held up, said, 'Put back your clothes, please!' I realised this had something to do with his being Muslim, but he was a treating me as if I were some sort of hooker propositioning him. 'But you're a doctor,' I said. 'How do female patients show you what's wrong with them?' He told me that a husband discreetly explains his wife's condition and then the doctor dispenses the appropriate medicine. I bought his medicine, which didn't work, and realised how very far away this world was from my own.

Laurie Gough, author of *Kiss the Sunset Pig*

Head for shelter

... if the weather turns bad, rather than carry on, hoping that it will improve. This may mean going back the way you came and not completing the trek, but severe weather in unknown places can be very dangerous and your safety should always be your priority.

Keep the airways clear

When trekking at high altitudes, smear a small amount of Vicks or similar product on your T-shirt. This will enable easier breathing by ensuring your air passages remain clear from obstruction.

TRAVEL FAUX PAS

IN BRAZIL THE HAND GESTURE USED IN THE WEST TO SIGNIFY 'OK' IS OFFENSIVE TO LOCALS.

Health and hygiene

Be sure to pack a good supply of sunscreen

... and after-sun lotion and take a brimmed hat. Sunburn is not only uncomfortable and unfashionable, but excessive exposure can be dangerous, leading to dehydration and sunstroke.

Make sure you drink enough water

... and have plenty with you when you are out and about. In hot countries you will need to drink a lot more water than you normally would do at home to avoid dehydration. If you wait until you are thirsty to drink, you are already dehydrated.

Err on the side of caution when it comes to drinking water

Buy bottled water or use water-purifying tablets if you are at all unsure about the quality of the tapwater, and expressly ask that no ice cubes be added when ordering drinks. If you don't have such commodities to hand, you can always boil any water you plan to drink.

Take hand sanitiser with you

There are many brands available that do not require water and will kill any nasty germs you have picked up along the way. Particularly handy for when you are just about to have a meal and there is no hand washing facility available. Remember: food poisoning does not just occur from eating badly prepared food.

Order piping hot food

... when eating out, rather than salads and raw vegetables, which may carry the bacteria that cause dysentery. If you are in any doubt of the state of meat on the menu then avoid it: badly cooked meat can leave you feeling unwell for days. A good rule to remember when it comes to food is 'peel it, cook it, boil it or forget it'.

TRAVEL TRIVIA

Although Australia has the largest number of living things anywhere in the world that can kill you, the largest killers in this antipodean country are actually skin cancer and heart disease.

If any creature bites you, seek medical attention immediately

Animals that you could safely assume are domestic in the UK may not be abroad. A lot of countries have a real problem with stray cats and dogs and it's safest not to approach or feed them. Apart from being less friendly than their pet counterparts, any painful bites that they might inflict on you could also transmit rabies. Remember that dogs aren't the only animals that can carry rabies: other carriers include bats, monkeys and rats.

In case of emergency

Always carry contact details

... for your embassy with you. The staff are there to help you, and will know the ins and outs of a country that is unfamiliar to you.

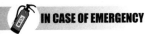

Never try and fight back

... or talk your way out of a situation if you are the victim of a violent theft or mugging. Similarly, don't cling on desperately to your bag or wallet. Your safety is much more important than your belongings.

Report it to the police immediately

... if you are robbed, and get a police report, as this will be needed for an insurance claim and will also help when replacing traveller's cheques and passport.

TRAVEL FAUX PAS

NEVER MAKE COMPARISONS BETWEEN BRAZILIAN AND ARGENTINIAN FOOTBALLERS: RIVALRIES ARE EXTREMELY STRONG, SO YOU COULD PROVOKE A DANGEROUSLY EXPLOSIVE DEBATE.

If your passport is lost or stolen, call your embassy

... and the airline you are travelling with immediately. Some airlines will permit you to travel with a police report and a photocopy of your passport or another form of photographic identification in the event that your passport has been stolen, but this is usually only within the EU and cannot be guaranteed.

Ask for a receipt

... if a police officer or other authority demands a fine for anything. If it is a large amount of money and the reasons behind the demand seem a little suspect, call your embassy. If you are driving, you may be pulled over by a police officer and asked for money – unfortunately there is little you can do in this situation, as they may well ask for your driving licence and refuse to hand it back until you have handed over some cash. In Asia, where this is perhaps most common, it might be an idea to hold less cash when you are driving in order to limit your losses.

Contact your embassy as soon as possible

... if you are arrested or get into trouble with the police, and they will send a representative to see you and offer advice on how to obtain legal assistance. However, remember that embassy staff will have very little sympathy if you are caught trafficking or possessing drugs. In some countries, drug possession carries serious long-term penalties and drug trafficking is punishable by death.

Call the Foreign Office in London

... or your embassy for advice in the event of a natural disaster or political turmoil that may be dangerous to your safety. Stay put unless you are in immediate danger, and only take essential items, such as your passport, wallet and valuables, with you if you have to move.

What to do in case of fire

- Sound the alarm if it is not already activated. If you have access to an extinguisher and it is a fairly small fire, try and put it out. However, if you feel that this would endanger your own safety, you are not able to use the extinguisher, or the fire is too large, exit the building as soon and as fast as possible. Do not stop to collect any belongings. If the fire prevents your exit remember these precautions until the fire department arrives:

- Smoke rises so stay low to the ground.

- Put a piece of clothing, towel or sheet over your mouth, wet if possible, to prevent smoke inhalation.

- Turn off the air conditioning, as the vents will bring more smoke into the room.

- Block gaps, underneath the door, for example, with wet material.

- Open the window slightly to attract outside attention and to have some fresh air to breathe, but do not open it fully as a rush of air into the room is likely to fan the flames and increase the fire.

Contact the British Embassy

... in cases of rape, violent crime or death whilst abroad. They can't become involved in any police investigation or any other legal matter, but they can provide advice and useful contacts.

TRAVEL FAUX PAS

BLEND IN ON THE BEACH IN RIO BY WEARING A SARONG INSTEAD OF BRINGING A TOWEL.

If you think you are lost, *stop*

Sit down, relax and don't panic. Look for landmarks and the position of the sun to orientate yourself. Do not start moving again until you work out where you are.

Stay in one place

... if you do get lost whilst hiking or trekking. This will aid the search party, which should be dispatched within 24 hours if you have given someone, perhaps hotel staff or fellow backpackers, your itinerary. Three short signals in quick succession, be it shouts, whistles or flashes of a torch, indicate an SOS distress call. Lighting a fire is another way of attracting attention, and of course is vital for warmth, but care should be taken when making fires in wooded areas, especially in very dry countries. If you believe that it is highly unlikely that a search party would have been alerted, you can try to find a source of water to follow downhill as this will usually lead to a settlement of some kind.

Be wary if someone offers you help after an accident

... or attempted robbery or assault. Some con artists will arrange for something like this to happen and then they or their partner will offer to 'help', which is actually just a front for stealing your possessions.

CASE STUDY

On our first morning in Bangkok a tuk-tuk driver offered to take my girlfriend and me to 'several temples' for about thirty pence. Naively, we accepted.

At the first temple a friendly Thai man told us he was praying for good luck on a journey he was taking. Apparently he took jewellery to the States and sold it for a massive profit.

'Jewellery is half price if you're a foreign national,' he claimed.

At temple number two another hit us with a similar story. The next stop was, oddly enough, a jewellery wholesalers.

We realised we were being conned, and got out of the situation by acting even more naive: 'Can we come again tomorrow when we've got money?'

The whole day was a great adventure, and I wouldn't change it for the world, but there was definitely a lesson to be learned – don't be naive! And if you realise you have been, not letting on and playing even dumber will usually get you out of it!

Tom Anderson, author of *Riding the Magic Carpet*

Stay positive

You've had your injections, booked your tickets, packed your bag and filled your head with useful advice and tips on how to stay safe on your travels. There is only one thing you can't prepare for: the unexpected. Inevitably, things won't go entirely smoothly for you during your travels, but the incidents and adventures you have and how you overcome them will probably be some of the things you remember most about your trip, and will make the best stories for telling to friends and family when you return home. With that in mind, here are a few final tips to help you stay positive and keep an open mind on your travels.

Take time to talk to the locals

Travelling is a wonderful opportunity to meet people you would never encounter at home and to engage with new cultures, so don't be suspicious of everyone you meet.

Take time to talk to other backpackers

Some of the best up-to-date advice on places to visit, what to avoid and local scams to be wary of in areas that you are visiting will come from fellow hostel residents. Swapping stories is also a great way to make new friends along the way. There are plenty of Internet notice boards where you can meet like-minded backpackers and get in touch with people going to the same areas that you plan to visit.

Try something new

One of the most disorientating and challenging things about travelling abroad is not having access to familiar food and finding people doing things very differently to what you are used to at home. If you are willing to sample a different kind of cuisine or go investigate a local festival, you will gain a lot more from the experience, and may even find you enjoy the new things that you try.

Be prepared to haggle

... and you could pick up some fantastic bargains. Medinas and street markets might be a pickpocket's haven, but they are also a bargain hunter's dream come true, so keep your wits about you and play the vendors at their own game.

Remember: it's an adventure

Don't take it too hard if things go wrong and learn to laugh about your mishaps and close shaves. After all, life would be boring if things always went according to plan.

Gap Year Adventures
A Guide to Making it a
Year to Remember

£3.99 Pb

Your gap year stretches ahead of you, begging to be filled with sun-drenched beaches, treks through exotic landscapes and thrilling exploits. How can you plan the adventures to make the most of your time out?

This essential guide is crammed with exciting ideas from around the world, from abseiling to zorbing, diving with sharks to learning yoga from the masters. Discover how to make your gap year truly unforgettable.

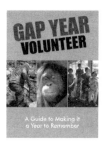

Gap Year Volunteer
A Guide to Making it a
Year to Remember

£3.99 Pb

You want to see the world – but you also want to help make it a better place. With so many aid opportunities on every continent, how do you find the one that's right for you?

Whether you want to care for tropical birds in Costa Rica, work with disadvantaged children in Morocco or raise money for research projects here in the UK, this handy book will answer all your volunteer questions, as well as offer inspiring ideas on what to do and where to go. Discover how to make your gap year truly unforgettable.

www.summersdale.com